Francis Frith's
Glasgow

Photographic Memories

Francis Frith's
Glasgow

Clive Hardy
&
Bill Bissett

Revised paperback edition published in the United Kingdom in 2000 by
Frith Book Company Ltd

First published in the United Kingdom in 1998
by WBC Ltd

British Library Cataloguing in Publication Data

Francis Frith's Glasgow & Clydeside
Clive Hardy

Revised Edition
Clive Hardy & Bill Bissett

ISBN 1-85937-190-6

Frith Book Company Ltd
Frith's Barn, Teffont,
Salisbury, Wiltshire SP3 5QP
Tel: +44 (0) 1722 716 376
Fax: +44 (0) 1722 716 881
Email: info@frithbook.co.uk
Web Site: www.frithbook.co.uk

Printed and bound in Great Britain

Front Cover: St. Vincent Place, Looking East 1896 39764

Contents

Francis Frith: *Victorian Pioneer*

FRANCIS FRITH, Victorian founder of the world-famous photographic archive, was a complex man. A devout Quaker and a highly successful Victorian businessman, he was both philosophic by nature and pioneering in outlook.

By 1855 Francis Frith had already established a wholesale grocery business in Liverpool, and sold it for the astonishing sum of £200,000, which is the equivalent today of over £15,000,000. Now a multi-millionaire, he was able to indulge his passion for travel. As a child he had pored over travel books written by early explorers, and his fancy and imagination had been stirred by family holidays to the sublime mountain regions of Wales and Scotland. 'What a land of spirit-stirring and enriching scenes and places!' he had written. He was to return to these scenes of grandeur in later years to 'recapture the thousands of vivid and tender memories', but with a different purpose. Now in his thirties, and captivated by the new science of photography, Frith set out on a series of pioneering journeys to the Nile regions that occupied him from 1856 until 1860.

Intrigue and Adventure

He took with him on his travels a specially-designed wicker carriage that acted as both dark-room and sleeping chamber. These far-flung journeys were packed with intrigue and adventure. In his life story, written when he was sixty-three, Frith tells of being held captive by bandits, and of fighting 'an awful midnight battle to the very point of surrender with a deadly pack of hungry, wild dogs'. Sporting flowing Arab costume, Frith arrived at Akaba by camel seventy years before Lawrence, where he encountered 'desert princes and rival sheikhs, blazing with jewel-hilted swords'.

During these extraordinary adventures he was assiduously exploring the desert regions bordering the Nile and patiently recording the antiquities and peoples with his camera. He was the first photographer to venture beyond the sixth cataract. Africa was still the mysterious 'Dark Continent', and Stanley and Livingstone's historic meeting was a decade into the future. The conditions for picture taking confound belief. He laboured for hours in his wicker dark-room in the sweltering heat of the desert, while the volatile chemicals fizzed dangerously in their trays. Often he was forced to work in remote tombs and caves where conditions were cooler. Back in London he exhibited his photographs and was 'rapturously cheered' by members of the Royal Society. His reputation as a photographer was made overnight. An eminent modern historian has likened their impact on the population of the time to that on our own generation of the first photographs taken on the surface of the moon.

Venture of a Life-Time

Characteristically, Frith quickly spotted the opportunity to create a new business as a specialist publisher of photographs. He lived in an era of immense and sometimes violent change. For the poor in the early part of Victoria's reign work was a drudge and the hours long, and people had precious little free time to enjoy themselves. Most had no transport other than a cart or gig at their disposal, and had not travelled far beyond the

boundaries of their own town or village. However, by the 1870s, the railways had threaded their way across the country, and Bank Holidays and half-day Saturdays had been made obligatory by Act of Parliament. All of a sudden the ordinary working man and his family were able to enjoy days out and see a little more of the world.

With characteristic business acumen, Francis Frith foresaw that these new tourists would enjoy having souvenirs to commemorate their days out. In 1860 he married Mary Ann Rosling and set out with the intention of photographing every city, town and village in Britain. For the next thirty years he travelled the country by train and by pony and trap, producing fine photographs of seaside resorts and beauty spots that were keenly bought by millions of Victorians. These prints were painstakingly pasted into family albums and pored over during the dark nights of winter, rekindling precious memories of summer excursions.

The Rise of Frith & Co

Frith's studio was soon supplying retail shops all over the country. To meet the demand he gathered about him a small team of photographers, and published the work of independent artist-photographers of the calibre of Roger Fenton and Francis Bedford. In order to gain some understanding of the scale of Frith's business one only has to look at the catalogue issued by Frith & Co in 1886: it runs to some 670 pages, listing not only many thousands of views of the British Isles but also many photographs of most European countries, and China, Japan, the USA and

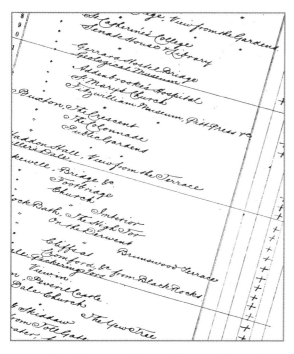

Canada – note the sample page shown above from the hand-written *Frith & Co* ledgers detailing pictures taken. By 1890 Frith had created the greatest specialist photographic publishing company in the world, with over 2,000 outlets – more than the combined number that Boots and WH Smith have today! The picture on the right shows the *Frith & Co* display board at Ingleton in the Yorkshire Dales. Beautifully constructed with mahogany frame and gilt inserts, it could display up to a dozen local scenes.

Postcard Bonanza

The ever-popular holiday postcard we know today took many years to develop. In 1870 the Post Office issued the first plain cards, with a pre-printed stamp on one face. In 1894 they allowed other publishers' cards to be sent through the mail with an attached adhesive halfpenny stamp. Demand grew rapidly, and

in 1895 a new size of postcard was permitted called the court card, but there was little room for illustration. In 1899, a year after Frith's death, a new card measuring 5.5 x 3.5 inches became the standard format, but it was not until 1902 that the divided back came into being, with address and message on one face and a full-size illustration on the other. *Frith & Co* were in the vanguard of postcard development, and Frith's sons Eustace and Cyril continued their father's monumental task, expanding the number of views offered to the public and recording more and more places in Britain, as the coasts and countryside were opened up to mass travel.

Francis Frith died in 1898 at his villa in Cannes, his great project still growing. The archive he created continued in business for another seventy years. By 1970 it contained over a third of a million pictures of 7,000 cities, towns and villages. The massive photographic record Frith has left to us stands as a living monument to a special and very remarkable man.

Frith's Archive: *A Unique Legacy*

FRANCIS FRITH'S legacy to us today is of immense significance and value, for the magnificent archive of evocative photographs he created provides a unique record of change in 7,000 cities, towns and villages throughout Britain over a century and more. Frith and his fellow studio photographers revisited locations many times down the years to update their views, compiling for us an enthralling and colourful pageant of British life and character.

We tend to think of Frith's sepia views of Britain as nostalgic, for most of us use them to conjure up memories of places in our own lives with which we have family associations. It often makes us forget that to Francis Frith they were records of daily life as it was actually being lived in the cities, towns and villages of his day. The Victorian age was one of great and often bewildering change for ordinary people, and though the pictures evoke an impression of slower times, life was as busy and hectic as it is today.

We are fortunate that Frith was a photographer of the people, dedicated to recording the minutiae of everyday life. For it is this sheer wealth of visual data, the painstaking chronicle of changes in dress, transport, street layouts, buildings, housing, engineering and landscape that captivates us so much today. His remarkable images offer us a powerful link with the past and with the lives of our ancestors.

Today's Technology

Computers have now made it possible for Frith's many thousands of images to be accessed almost instantly. In the Frith archive today, each photograph is carefully 'digitised' then stored on a CD Rom. Frith archivists can locate a single photograph amongst thousands within seconds. Views can be catalogued and sorted under a variety of categories of place and content to the immediate benefit of researchers.

Inexpensive reference prints can be created for them at the touch of a mouse button, and a wide range of books and other printed materials assembled and published for a wider, more general readership - in the next twelve months over a hundred Frith local history titles will be published! The day-to-day workings of the archive are very different from how they were in Francis Frith's time: imagine the herculean task of sorting through eleven tons of glass negatives as Frith had to do to locate a particular

See Frith at www. frithbook.co.uk

sequence of pictures! Yet the archive still prides itself on maintaining the same high standards of excellence laid down by Francis Frith, including the painstaking cataloguing and indexing of every view.

It is curious to reflect on how the internet now allows researchers in America and elsewhere greater instant access to the archive than Frith himself ever enjoyed. Many thousands of individual views can be called up on screen within seconds on one of the Frith internet sites, enabling people living continents away to revisit the streets of their ancestral home town, or view places in Britain where they have enjoyed holidays. Many overseas researchers welcome the chance to view special theme selections, such as transport, sports, costume and ancient monuments.

We are certain that Francis Frith would have heartily approved of these modern developments in imaging techniques, for he himself was always working at the very limits of Victorian photographic technology.

The Value of the Archive Today

Because of the benefits brought by the computer, Frith's images are increasingly studied by social historians, by researchers into genealogy and ancestory, by architects, town planners, and by teachers and schoolchildren involved in local history projects.

In addition, the Frith archive offers every one of us a unique opportunity to examine the places where we and our families have lived and worked down the years. Immensely successful in Frith's own era, the archive is now, a century and more on, entering a new phase of popularity.

The Past in Tune with the Future

Historians consider the Francis Frith Collection to be of prime national importance. It is the only archive of its kind remaining in private ownership and has been valued at a million pounds. However, this figure is now rapidly increasing as digital technology enables more and more people around the world to enjoy its benefits.

Francis Frith's archive is now housed in an historic timber barn in the beautiful village of Teffont in Wiltshire. Its founder would not recognize the archive office as it is today. In place of the many thousands of dusty boxes containing glass plate negatives and an all-pervading odour of photographic chemicals, there are now ranks of computer screens. He would be amazed to watch his images travelling round the world at unimaginable speeds through network and internet lines.

The archive's future is both bright and exciting. Francis Frith, with his unshakeable belief in making photographs available to the greatest number of people, would undoubtedly approve of what is being done today with his lifetime's work. His photographs, depicting our shared past, are now bringing pleasure and enlightenment to millions around the world a century and more after his death.

Looking along the Broomielaw towards Clyde Street, 1897 39801
The picture gives us a good view of the railway bridge
serving Central Station, whilst immediately behind it work is underway
on rebuilding Glasgow Bridge. It is also possible to
make out the towers of the suspension bridge situated a little further
along the river. On the far bank are some of the
warehouses along Bridge Wharf.

Glasgow

With its Cathedral founded in 1136, and the University founded in 1451, by the mid 15th century Glasgow was little-known outside Scotland, and then only as a place of learning and Christian culture.

The advent of overseas trade, particularly with the American colonies, resulted in textile and tobacco businesses flourishing in the 18th century. The geographical advantage of Glasgow's position straddling the river Clyde meant that the Industrial Revolution in the following century witnessed the huge expansion of heavy engineering, steel and ironworks, shipbuilding, and locomotive steam engines.

This in turn led to a great population increase, and this rapid growth brought with it many social problems. The existing schools, housing, medical services, water supply, and sanitary arrangements were totally inadequate for the needs of the people. Remedial action was taken by the City Council, not all of it being for the better, because the programme of housing left a legacy of slums and health problems which had to be tackled in later years. However, the Loch Katrine water supply scheme, opened by Queen Victoria in 1859, is one example of magnificent forward planning. There will never be any shortage of water in Glasgow. The recreational needs of the people had to be met, and Glasgow became famous for its many public parks, theatres, and music-halls. By the latter half of the 19th century Glasgow had become 'the second city of the Empire'.

▼ **Glasgow, at The Broomielaw 1897** 39799
The Glasgow & Inverary and the Lochgoil & Lochlong Steamboat
Companies sported the same colour scheme. Black hull and paddle
boxes with white saloons and lifeboats. The funnel colour was red,
with two white bands enclosing a black one. The top of the funnel
was also painted black.

▼ **Glasgow, St Enochs Hotel 1897** 39792

▲ **Buchanan Street
1897** 39767
This street is mostly
now pedestrianised,
with a large variety of
shops to suit all
tastes. The
architecture is
interesting, including
the Stock Exchange,
and St George's Tron
Church. On the site
of the former railway
station there has
recently opened the
Buchanan Galleries,
an indoor shopping
complex.

◄ **Glasgow,
Municipal Buildings 1897**
39760
It used to be said that George
Square reminded visiting
Londoners of Trafalgar Square,
except that the central column
was a monument to Sir Walter
Scott instead of Lord Nelson. The
Square served to emphasise
Glasgow's self-proclaimed
status as 'the second city of the
Empire.' Here were the
magnificent municipal buildings,
completed in 1888 at a cost of
£540,000, including the post
office, the Bank of Scotland, the
Merchant's House and
several hotels.

Argyle Street 1897
39765
We are at the corner with Union Street. This is still a very busy and popular shopping area, largely pedestrianised. The last tramcars were withdrawn in September 1962, but examples can be seen at the Transport Museum in the Kelvin Hall along with very many other exhibits.

◄ **Glasgow,
Municipal Buildings
1897** 39761

◀ Renfield Street 1897
39769
Renfield Street is now part of the one-way system (south-bound). Today it is still thronged with people, but there is not a tramline to be seen; although on many of the buildings throughout the city the anchoring hooks for the tramway overhead wires are evident.

▼ George Square 1897 39759
In the centre of the square the column of Sir Walter Scott dominates. The large building in the centre background is the Merchants' House, opened in 1877. Upper storeys have since been added. There are many statues of famous Victorian figures, including the only equestrian statue of Queen Victoria ever made. Prince Albert (also on horseback) is nearby.

◀ Glasgow, The Stock Exchange 1897 39771
The Stock Exchange was yet another symbol of Glasgow's industrial might.

**Sauchiehall Street
1897** 39763
We are looking west.
This part is now
pedestrianised. Most of
the buildings shown
here have gone, and
there is a large indoor
shopping complex and
car parking facilities
where the clock tower
appears. There are still
many high-quality
shops in this
famous street.

St. Vincent Place, Looking East 1897 39764
Here, within the heartland of the majority of commercial and financial institutions, the imposing buildings are still standing, and even the public conveniences, in the right foreground, still exist! In the hazy background of the photograph can be seen the right-hand domed part of the City Chambers in George Square.

Glasgow, The Royal Exchange 1897 39798
The Royal Exchange was built in the Corinthian style. It was one of the many buildings which symbolised Glasgow's industrial and economic status. At the beginning of the nineteenth century, only one Scot in twenty lived in Glasgow. By the end of the century the figure was one in five.

Charing Cross 1897 39768
This view shows the Grand Hotel and Charing Cross Mansions in the background. The Mansions still exist, but the hotel was demolished to make way for the M8 motorway Kingston Bridge crossing over the Clyde at this point.

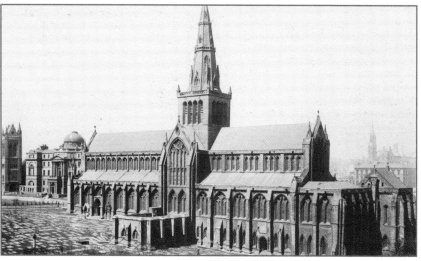

◄ **Glasgow Cathedral
and Necropolis 1897**
39775

◀ **The Cathedral 1897** 39774
Founded in 1136, on the site of St Mungo's Church of 543AD, the Cathedral has gone through many times of peace and of strife. On one door in the Cathedral lead shot can still be seen; it bears witness to the citizens' successful defence against the Reformation zealots who would have destroyed it. The 'Bridge of Sighs' in the foreground leads to the Eastern Necropolis. The Royal Infirmary, designed by Robert and James Adam in 1792, is on the immediate left of the Cathedral. It was there that Lord Joseph Lister first began antiseptic treatment and Dr John Macintyre was the first to use X-rays for diagnosis.

▼ **Glasgow Cathedral and Necropolis 1890**
G11001
Another view of the cathedral. Behind the cathedral, the Necropolis can be seen, stretching from the left and to the right of the photograph.

◀ **Glasgow Cathedral and Crypt 1897** 39783
Below the choir is the crypt, part of which dates from 1197 when it was consecrated by Bishop Jocelin. It is well proportioned with fine pillars and vaulting. In the centre of the crypt is the site of the tomb of St Kentigern (St Mungo) and it was over his grave that the first church was erected.

Glasgow Cathedral and Choir East 1897 39780
The choir dates from the thirteenth century and contains a superb fifteenth century stone screen. Behind the choir are the Chapter House, which has a richly carved doorway, and the Lady Chapel. In the Chapter House is a gravestone to the memory of nine martyred Covenanters.

Glasgow Cathedral and Choir West 1897 39779
Looking west from the choir towards the nave. Glasgow Cathedral survives almost intact and is said to be the most complete in Scotland, having lost only its western towers which were dismantled during the nineteenth century.

Glasgow Cathedral and Nave East 1897 39778

The nave with its timbered ceiling was completed in 1480. At a later date it was divided into three congregations, the nave, choir and crypt. In this picture from 1897, we can see the screen separating the nave and choir. During the nineteenth century the windows throughout the church were filled with stained glass, most of it from Munich, at a cost close to £100,000.

Glasgow Necropolis 1897 39784

The Victorian celebration of death. This is the Necropolis situated behind the cathedral, containing a number of substantial monuments to the great and the good, and to those who simply had enough money to build. The large statue is to the memory of the reformer John Knox.

▼ Glasgow Royal Infirmary 1897 39789

The Royal Infirmary, next door to the cathedral and just a hearse's ride away from the Necropolis. At this time nearly 430,000 people were crammed into central Glasgow, and the city's tenement blocks were a breeding ground for all manner of contagious diseases.

▼ Glasgow Western Infirmary 1897 39788

The imposing front of the Western Infirmary. Between 1861 and 1881 the city experienced four major cholera epidemics. To add to this rickets and tuberculosis were endemic amongst mill workers and smallpox was rife. During this period, a quarter of all children born to mill workers died before reaching their first birthday.

▲ Glasgow Botanical Gardens 1897 39796

The Kibble Palace which was re-erected in the gardens in 1872 now houses rare tree ferns. Both William Gladstone and the Earl of Beaconsfield used the building to deliver their rectorial addresses to members of the university.

The Botanic Gardens 1897 39795

The Botanic Gardens occupy 43 acres off Great Western Road, and many orchids, tropical plants and trees are grown in the conservatories. The Kibble Palace, the largest glasshouse in Britain, is now a Winter Garden, but was formerly used for public meetings and concerts. Disraeli (Earl Beaconsfield) and Gladstone delivered their Rectorial addresses to the Glasgow University students under its immense dome.

Paisley

Paisley has many historical connections. It is famous for the 'Paisley pattern' shawls which were the height of European fashion during most of the 19th century. Paisley Abbey, a Cluniac monastery founded in 1163 and now a charge of the Church of Scotland, has much 14th- and 15th-century architecture and stained-glass windows. Coats Observatory, built in 1882, is one of the best-equipped in Britain and has regular guided tours. The central area of the town has been completely redesigned with pedestrian-only shopping malls and a one-way traffic system.

Paisley, High Street 1900
45993
Most of the scene in the picture has become pedestrianised only recently. The majority of the buildings on the right are still standing, but many on the left have gone to make way for new stores. Further along the street is the opulent Thomas Coats Memorial Church, built and endowed by the famous Paisley weaving family.

Paisley, Dunn Square 1901 47398
Dunn Square is a haven of tranquil peace amidst the bustle of a busy town centre. The statues, including those of Queen Victoria, and of Robert Tannahill, the weaver and poet who was born in Paisley, still adorn this square, although the layout has been altered since this photograph was taken.

Paisley, Crookston Castle 1897 39808
It was to here that Mary Queen of Scots and Henry, Lord Darnley came following their marriage in July 1565. The castle was owned by Henry's father, the Earl of Lennox. This was the first property to be acquired by the National Trust for Scotland.

Paisley, The Burns Memorial 1900 45996
Born at Alloway, Ayrshire in 1759, Burns' love of poetry was instilled in him by his teacher, John Murdoch. Burns died of rheumatic fever in 1796, contracting it after falling asleep by the roadside on his way home from a heavy drinking session.

Greenock

Greenock was a beneficiary of the River Clyde's industrial heyday. It is sad that most of the shipbuilding and heavy industry have gone into decline. The first square-rigger to be built was launched here in 1760. However, there are still sugar refining and textile works existing. James Watt, the great engineer who pioneered the steam engine, was born here. Near the West Pier is the West Kirk, the first church to be built after the Reformation and relocated on this site. On a hill viewpoint just outside the town is a Cross of Lorraine with an anchor, which is a memorial to the Free French sailors who gave their lives in the Second World War during the Battle of the Atlantic.

Greenock, Customs House Quay 1897 39814 Greenock Custom House was built in 1818. In the distance are Cartsdyke mill and east yards, the Gravel graving dock and the entrance to the James Watt Dock.

Greenock, From Whinhill 1899 43400
This view, looks out over the smoking chimney pots of Greenock and across the Firth of Clyde to the entrance to Gare Loch.

Greenock, The Courthouse 1897 39818
A busy place at times, considering that imprisonment for being drunk and incapable were running at 300 a month in Glasgow alone. Between 1872-4 there were around 125,000 arrests on drink charges throughout Scotland. In 1900 Provost Black of Greenock, a strict temperance man, wanted legislation introduced to close ice-cream shops on a Sunday. Black considered that people enjoying themselves by eating ice-cream were not behaving in a proper manner on the Sabbath.

Greenock from The Harbour 1904 52632

During the late seventeenth century Greenock's trade in herrings with France and the Baltic required a fleet of over 300 boats. The town motto was 'Let herring swim that trade maintain'. The herring went elsewhere and the trade declined.

Gourock

On the Firth of Clyde, this seaside resort looks across the Firth towards Kilcreggan, Loch Long and Dunoon. It is a centre for yachting and for boating trips in the Firth and to the Kyles of Bute. On the cliff side of Gourock is a prehistoric monolith, Granny Kempock's Stone, which is still associated with ancient myths and is given superstitious respect. There are splendid views over the resort and estuary from Gourock Golf Club, which is situated high above the town.

Gourock and The Clyde 1900 45962
There is plenty of activity on the railway and at the pier. In the distance is Kilcreggan on the Rosneath peninsula, and the entrance to Loch Long which is backed by the Cowal hills.

◄ **Gourock, Kempock Place in 1900** 45977
The entrance to the pier for the Dunoon boats is to the right.

◄ Gourock from Tower Hill 1900 45965

A view over the rooftops from Tower Hill. The steamer crossing West Bay is turning to berth at the pier. A steamer has just departed possibly heading for Glasgow.

▼ Gourock from the pier in 1900 45975

This View shows the backs of buildings along Kempock Street. Kempock Place is just in view on the extreme left of the picture. Over to the right is Seaton's Temperance Hotel, one of several in the town. At this time temperance hotels abounded throughout the UK, but there was in fact little difference between them and private hotels, as neither had liquor licences.

◄ Gourock, Barrhill Road 1900 45979

In the background are the castle mansions and the Free Church. To the right behind the houses is Tower Hill, the site of Gourock Castle. Built in 1747 the castle was demolished before the Great War.

**Gourock,
The Esplanade 1900**
45969
The esplanade with the
pebble beach in
evidence. As well as
being a resort, Gourock
was noted for its
herring curing. In 1688
the first recorded curing
of red herrings took
place here.

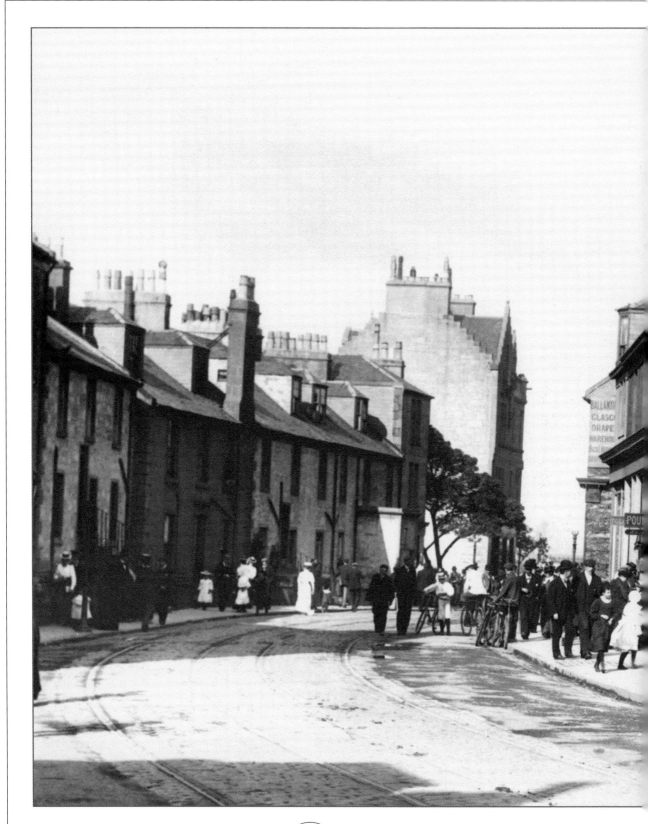

Gourock, Kempock Street 1900 45978 Kempock Street is a popular street of many shops and dwellings near the pier and ferry terminal. It has become a focal point for day-trippers and tourists. The Victorian scene shown here has given way to a busy thoroughfare. Although there are tramlines, the service did not become electrified until 1901-1902. The part building on the immediate left of the picture - Veitch's Temperance Hotel - was renamed some years later, and was demolished in the 1950s as the result of a fire.

▼ **Gourock, Haddon's Temperance Hotel 1900** 45985
John Dunlop, a local lawyer was one of the leading lights in the
Clydeside temperance movement, founding the first society in the
1820s. By 1876 the Independent Order of Good Templars had
84,000 members in Scotland.

▼ **Gourock, Cloch Point and Pilot's Cottage 1900** 45987
During the Second World War an anti-submarine boom ran across the
river from Cloch Point to the Gantocks. Additional defenses comprised
fixed gun positions at Cloch Point, Toward Point and on Castle
Hill, Dunoon.

▲ **Cloch Point, The
Lighthouse 1900** 45986
The lighthouse between
Gourock and Inverkip.
Built in 1796, the
lighthouse stands 76 ft
high and is a notable
Clyde estuary landmark,
looking across to the light
on the Gantock rocks.

◀ **Inverkip Valley 1899** 43411
The village used to be called Auldkirk because the people of Greenock worshipped here until they built their own church at the end of the sixteenth century. In 1640 witch mania was rife throughout Scotland. The General Assembly instructed ministers to 'take notice of witches, charmers and all such abusers of the people'. Inverkip joined in the burnings, becoming a notorious centre for following the Bible's demand that, 'Thou shalt not suffer a witch to live'.

Clydebank

In 1871 only a farmhouse occupied the site. By 1872 a shipyard ,which had moved from Govan in Glasgow, had become established; as the site had no name, the shipyard managers decided on the name 'Clydebank'. That same year its first ship was launched. In 1884 the Singer Manufacturing Company from America set up a sewing-machine factory; the Singer's clock tower was a landmark in Clydebank for many years until it was demolished. By then, a large working township had developed from that farm site. The shipbuilding company of John Brown, who moved here from Sheffield when they took over James and George Thomson's Shipyard in 1899, built many famous liners; these included the 'Lusitania', launched in 1906, the 'Queen Mary', launched in 1934, the 'Queen Elizabeth', launched in 1938, and the 'Queen Elizabeth II', launched in 1967. In March 1941, during the Second World War, Clydebank was almost totally destroyed by bombing, suffering more than the Coventry raids. Only seven houses in the burgh were undamaged, over 4,300 were destroyed or damaged beyond repair, and whole families were wiped out. John Brown's shipyard, the main target, was able to continue production. It is sad that today many of these works have gone, but Clydebank continues to thrive as an active burgh.

Clydebank, Town Hall under construction 1900
C208003
The streets are packed with onlookers, and anxious officials wait by the entrance to the site of the new town hall. During the Second World War, Clydebank, given its size suffered the heaviest bombing in Britain. Only seven houses escaped damage, thousands were destroyed or damaged beyond repair and many were hit more than once.

Clydebank, Glasgow Road 1900 C208004
Many of these buildings were built by Thomson for their shipyard workers. Some still exist, but many houses have been replaced by new buildings.

Beardmore Terrace, Dalmuir c1900 C208001
The Beardmore family were partners in the Parkhead forge and later acquired the Govan East shipyard. The Dalmuir yard was opened in 1905 primarily to build warships, the Govan workforce transferring to the new site. The first ship to be completed was the Zaza, a private yacht for William Beardmore.

Clydebank, Glasgow Road c1900 C208005
Here we see another view of this main road. The tramway system in Clydebank was operated by Glasgow Corporation, and on certain routes in this burgh single-deck trams had to be used to enable them to negotiate the low railway bridges.

Clydebank, Kilbowie Road 1900 C208002
In 1890 only the building on the left existed. This was built by Singer to house their workers. The right-hand side was tree-lined. By 1900 the tenements appear; their gable-ends were obviously a popular advertising site. A workman on a ladder can be seen altering one of the advertisements - one wonders how high his ladder can reach. The congested canal bridge in the picture was replaced by a metal swingbridge in 1916, after very heated and protracted meetings between Glasgow Corporation and Clydebank Burgh regarding responsibility for the cost. The new bridge allowed trams to travel beyond Clydebank to Duntocher; the fare from Kilbowie Road to Duntocher was all of a halfpenny!

Helensburgh & Gare Loch

Founded in 1776 by Sir James Colquhoun of Luss, who named the town after his wife, Helensburgh has become popular as a holiday resort and for golfing, fishing and a yachting centre. It stands on the Lower Clyde near the entrance to Gareloch. Henry Bell, who became a Provost of the burgh, designed and built the steamboat 'Comet'; an obelisk to him is on the Esplanade, and the flywheel from the 'Comet' is preserved in Hermitage Park. The Scottish engineer John Logie Baird (1888-1946), pioneer of television, was born here. One of his original sets is in the local library. In Upper Colquhoun Street is Hill House, an Edwardian villa designed by Charles Rennie Mackintosh, the famous architect. It is now owned by the National Trust for Scotland.

**Helensburgh,
The Esplanade 1901**
47402
There are still ample shops, cafes and restaurants here, and most of the buildings still exist. Car-parking facilities have been provided. The memorial column to Henry Bell can be seen near the pier. The clock tower has been incorporated in the tourist information office.

▼ **Helensburgh in 1897** 39811
Helensburgh was described as '. . . a favourite watering place, is
pleasantly situated at the mouth of the Gareloch, and is laid out with
the mathematical regularity of an American city.'

▼ **Helensburgh, Warship 1901** 47416
By 1901 warships from the age of sail had long ceased to have any
operational value. However, a surprising number from the 1840s and 50s
still survived. Many had been reduced to storage hulks, but others served as
accommodation ships, base and headquarters ships and as training vessels.

▲ **Helensburgh
Esplanade 1901** 47484
Here we have a good
view of the beach, sea
wall and the grassed-over
area where trippers could
sit and relax. Beyond are
the Esplanade shops
and cafes.

◄ **Helensburgh and Rhu from the peir 1901** 47415 Henry Bell, the pioneer of steam navigation in Europe is buried in the churchyard at Rhu. In 1812 Bell launched the steamboat Comet on the Clyde, where it operated until 1820.

◀ **Dunoon Sandbanks and Holy Loch 1901**
47428
This is the village of Sandbank on the western side of Holy Loch. On the far side are the houses of Kilmun and the heights of Stronchullin Hill, Beinn Ruadh and Creachan Mor.

Cowal
Holy Loch

Holy Loch 1897 39849
Holy Loch is little more than a small inlet the Clyde estuary. In the 1960s however, this quiet backwater became internationally famous when it was chosen as a base for the United States Navy nuclear submarine force. The picture dates from 1897, when submarines were still very much in the experimental stage.

◀ **Holy Loch 1901** 47427
The village of Sandbank is on the left, Kilmun is off camera to the right. Kilmun is the burial place of the Marquis of Argyll who was executed in 1661, whilst in the churchyard there is the tombstone of Archibald Clark, a young shepherd, who was found frozen to death at Ardtaric in September 1854.

Dunoon

Since the 1850s, Dunoon has always been a favourite resort for Glaswegians. The 'doon the watter' trips from the Broomielaw in Glasgow became almost an institution from then until the Second World War. Today, ferries from Gourock still ply their trade. Dunoon was also a place of residence for many American naval personnel, whose submarine base was until recently in the Holy Loch. During the last weekend of every August the Cowal Highland Gathering is held, which provides two days of Highland Games; on the Saturday the spectacle of pipe bands from all over the world can be seen as they march along the main street to Cowal. Robert Burns's 'Highland Mary' - Mary Campbell - was born locally; a statue to her is on the hillside. They intended to marry, and emigrate to the West Indies, but she took ill and died, and Burns in his grief decided to remain in Scotland.

Dunoon Pier 1904 52618
Dunoon Pier devoid of shipping. During the early 1880s problems with drunken Glaswegians running amok in the coastal towns, had led to the withdrawal of Sunday excursion sailings. With pubs in Glasgow being shut on the Sabbath, the only place to get a drink had been onboard an excursion steamer.

Dunoon, The Pier 1904 52620
The buildings and the pier have been modernised to cope with today's holiday traffic demands. The steamers now trading between the resorts all belong to the one company only, Caledonian MacBrayne, who operate all services on the west coast of Scotland and the Western Isles.

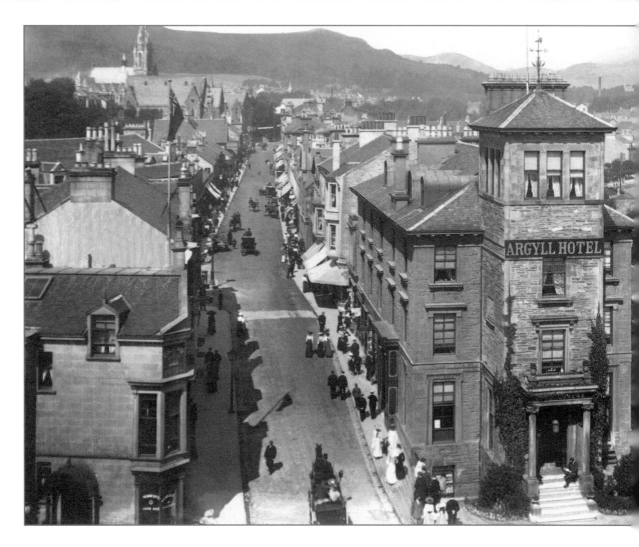

◀ **Dunoon, Columba 1904**

52621

The MacBrayne steamer Columba picks up speed as she pulls away from Dunoon. Built in 1878 and flagship of the MacBrayne fleet, Columba was renowned for the quality of her passenger comfort, with saloons the full width of her hull, a barber's shop and a post office. When first commissioned, she was placed on the up-market daily run from Glasgow to Tarbert and Ardrishaig, by way of Greenock, Dunoon, Rothesay and the Kyles of Bute.

Dunoon, Argyll Hotel, Main Street 1904 52614

This view was taken from Castle Hill looking north. The Argyll Hotel continues to attract guests, and the scene today is much as is shown here, except for the fashions and the absence of horses. The view looks toward Cowal, and it is mandatory that every Pipe Band which takes part in the Cowal Games held each August must march from the Castle gardens along the street to Cowal, playing most of the way; it is a most stirring sight.

Dunoon Castle 1897

39831

Visitors clamber over the site of the old castle. The modern castle is comparatively new, being completed in 1822. The statue is of Burns's Highland Mary, who was born at Auchnamore Farm nearby. The statue was erected in 1896.

Dunoon, Castle Gardens 1897 39832

The Gardens at Dunoon offer a little peace and tranquillity, compared to the hustle and bustle of the town. The picture might have been taken on a Sunday; it was at the time when the Clyde excursion steamers did not sail on the Sabbath.

Dunoon 1904 52613
Sunday trippers make their way from the pier to Argyll Street. Dunoon being the largest and best known of the Cowal resorts, its main steamer links were with Gourock, Rothesay and with the North British Railway at Raigendoran. It was also an interchange for those passengers wishing to take the Oban steamer.

Dunoon, West Bay 1897 39829
Children play on the beach and paddle in the sea, whilst their mums have the chance to knit while they natter. In the days before deckchairs, was it possible to hire benches to sit on?

Dunoon Castle Hill 1904 52616
A 1904 view of the pier esplanade, castle rock and the new castle. There were no trams serving Dunoon, but there were a number of horse-drawn omnibuses working between the West and East Bays. One of them is just in this picture on the extreme right.

◄ **Dunoon,
West Bay 1901** 47421
Local fisherman work on
their boat; the large
piece of material on the
beach is probably the
sail. A popular place for
a paddle, though none
of the Frith Collection
pictures show any
bathing machines, which
were such a feature of
the English resorts.

◄ **Dunoon,
West Bay 1904** 52615
The group of people on the left appear to be on a well prepared outing and are having a picnic. The small huts are where you hired your boat from, for a by-the-hour row round the bay.

▼ **Dunoon,
East Bay 1901** 47418
looking towards Kirn and Hunter's Quay. Hunter's Quay became the headquarters for the Clyde Yachting Club, and the annual Clyde Yachting Fortnight. It gets its name from the Hunter family of Hafton House.

◄ **Dunoon River 1901**
47425
Dunoon from the high ground behind the town. Inland to the west, the moorland rises to over 1,600 ft, the highest point being known as the Bishop's Seat.

The Kyles of Bute
Rothersay

The first effective spinning mill in the West of Scotland was built at Rothesay. Between 1787 and 1834, the number of cotton mills opened in Scotland rocketed from just 19 to 134. During the American Civil War imports of cotton fell from 8,600 tons in 1861, to 500 tons in 1862 and 350 tons in 1864. The effects of the naval blockade by the North on Confederate ports caused severe distress and hardship amongst British mill workers.

**Rothesay Pier
from Chapel Hill 1900**
45990

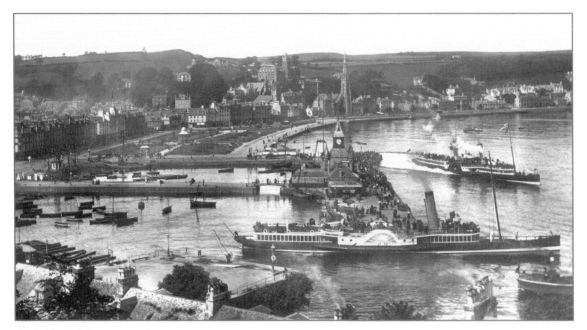

Rothesay, The Pier 1897 39836
Rothesay is the county town on the eastern side of the Island of Bute, in an ideal location in the sheltered 'sweet Rothesay Bay', to quote the popular song. The pier has changed little from the way it looks in this photograph: in the holiday period it is still as busy as it was a century ago. The main sailing destinations from here are to Wemyss Bay on the Ayrshire coast and, in the summer season, to the Island of Arran, as well as holiday excursions.

Rothesay, The Castle 1897 39845
The partly-restored moated 13th-century castle was once one of the regular residences of the Scottish kings. In 1398, Robert III created his eldest son Duke of Rothesay, and to this day the heir to the throne retains this as one of his titles - Prince Charles is the current holder. The castle is imposingly situated in the town centre, above the bay, and was originally circular in plan with four towers.

Rothesay, The Esplanade 1897 39838
The wide sweep of the Esplanade in this Victorian scene is almost unchanged, with the exception of the tramway system and the railings along the gardens. This is still a very popular tourist resort which provides all types of amenities for the visitor.

Rothesay Esplanade, Looking North 1897

39837.

The tram and tramlines are gone now, but the buildings and the main hotels still exist. The Victorian elegance has given way to more casual fashions, and horse-drawn vehicles have all but disappeared. The pier continues to cater for steamer excursions, and there are ample opportunities for the sea angler. The town also has winter gardens, a swimming pool, dancing, and golf, to name only a few of the attractions in this pleasant resort.

▼ **Rothesay Castle 1897** 39844
Part of the circular courtyard of the thirteenth century castle; a
favourite spot with Victorian visitors for a picnic. On the left can be
seen the honeycomb internal stonework of one of the turrets.

▼ **Rothesay, Ardbeg Point & Cowal Hill 1897** 39843A
This is Ardbeg Point, with Loch Striven in the distance. The entrance to
the Kyles of Bute is just beyond the headland.

▲ **Rothesay, The
Esplanade 1897** 39840

◀ **Rothersay, Loch Fad 1904** 52610
Loch Fad is the largest inland stretch of water on Bute. On the western shore stands the regency-style house built in 1827 by the actor Edmund Kean.

Largs

The battle of Largs, famous in Scottish history, took place in 1263; victory went to the Scots, which put paid to any attempts by Norwegian Vikings to dominate. Every year in September Largs, with active enthusiasm from the Norwegians, holds a Viking Festival; this includes parades, bonfires, and music. Largs is a popular holiday resort and sporting centre, and its sheltered waters are an attraction for yachting and other sailing sports. The town has many amenities to appeal to tourists; the resort has redesigned its seafront and provided facilities for the holidaymaker and day-tripper. There is an interesting recently-opened Viking museum, and Nardini's famous ice-cream parlour is eagerly enjoyed by the visitors.

Largs, The Esplanade 1897 39856
The buildings in this scene are still recognisable, although they have been renovated and modernised. The Esplanade has been landscaped, with grassy greens, paved walkways, plenty of seating, and leisure amenities. New houses have also been erected nearby. St Columba's Parish Church is still a landmark.

Largs, The Pier 1897 39851
This is the embarkation point for sailings to the various Clyde resorts, and also to Millport, just across from and within sight of Largs, on the island of Great Cumbrae. The pier is little changed today. The lower building to the immediate right of the Temperance Hotel was a public house, the Old Pier Vaults, an interesting combination!

Sunset on the Clyde in 1897 39825

Index

Frith Book Co Titles

www.frithbook.co.uk

The Frith Book Company publishes over 100 new titles each year. A selection of those currently available are listed below. For latest catalogue please contact Frith Book Co.

Town Books 96pp, 100 photos. County and Themed Books 128pp, 150 photos (unless specified). All titles hardback laminated case and jacket except those indicated pb (paperback)

Around Bakewell	1-85937-113-2	£12.99	English Castles	1-85937-078-0	£14.99
Around Barnstaple	1-85937-084-5	£12.99	Essex	1-85937-082-9	£14.99
Around Bath	1-85937-097-7	£12.99	Around Exeter	1-85937-126-4	£12.99
Around Belfast	1-85937-094-2	£12.99	Exmoor	1-85937-132-9	£14.99
Berkshire (pb)	1-85937-191-4	£9.99	Around Falmouth	1-85937-066-7	£12.99
Around Blackpool	1-85937-049-7	£12.99	Around Great Yarmouth	1-85937-085-3	£12.99
Around Bognor Regis	1-85937-055-1	£12.99	Greater Manchester	1-85937-108-6	£14.99
Around Bournemouth	1-85937-067-5	£12.99	Around Guildford	1-85937-117-5	£12.99
Brighton (pb)	1-85937-192-2	£8.99	Hampshire	1-85937-064-0	£14.99
Around Bristol	1-85937-050-0	£12.99	Around Harrogate	1-85937-112-4	£12.99
British Life A Century Ago	1-85937-103-5	£17.99	Around Horsham	1-85937-127-2	£12.99
Buckinghamshire (pb)	1-85937-200-7	£9.99	Around Ipswich	1-85937-133-7	£12.99
Around Cambridge	1-85937-092-6	£12.99	Ireland (pb)	1-85937-181-7	£9.99
Cambridgeshire	1-85937-086-1	£14.99	Isle of Man	1-85937-065-9	£14.99
Canals and Waterways	1-85937-129-9	£17.99	Isle of Wight	1-85937-114-0	£14.99
Cheshire	1-85937-045-4	£14.99	Kent (pb)	1-85937-189-2	£9.99
Around Chester	1-85937-090-x	£12.99	Around Leicester	1-85937-073-x	£12.99
Around Chesterfield	1-85937-071-3	£12.99	Leicestershire (pb)	1-85937-185-x	£9.99
Around Chichester	1-85937-089-6	£12.99	Around Lincoln	1-85937-111-6	£12.99
Churches of Berkshire	1-85937-170-1	£17.99	Lincolnshire	1-85937-135-3	£14.99
Churches of Dorset	1-85937-172-8	£17.99	Around Liverpool	1-85937-051-9	£12.99
Colchester (pb)	1-85937-188-4	£8.99	London (pb)	1-85937-183-3	£9.99
Cornwall	1-85937-054-3	£14.99	Around Maidstone	1-85937-056-x	£12.99
Cotswolds	1-85937-099-3	£14.99	New Forest	1-85937-128-0	£14.99
Cumbria	1-85937-101-9	£14.99	Around Newark	1-85937-105-1	£12.99
Dartmoor	1-85937-145-0	£14.99	Around Newquay	1-85937-140-x	£12.99
Around Derby	1-85937-046-2	£12.99	North Devon Coast	1-85937-146-9	£14.99
Derbyshire (pb)	1-85937-196-5	£9.99	North Yorkshire	1-85937-048-9	£14.99
Devon	1-85937-052-7	£14.99	Northumberland and Tyne & Wear		
Dorset	1-85937-075-6	£14.99		1-85937-072-1	£14.99
Dorset Coast	1-85937-062-4	£14.99	Norwich (pb)	1-85937-194-9	£8.99
Down the Severn	1-85937-118-3	£14.99	Around Nottingham	1-85937-060-8	£12.99
Down the Thames	1-85937-121-3	£14.99	Nottinghamshire (pb)	1-85937-187-6	£9.99
Around Dublin	1-85937-058-6	£12.99	Around Oxford	1-85937-096-9	£12.99
East Anglia	1-85937-059-4	£14.99	Oxfordshire	1-85937-076-4	£14.99
East Sussex	1-85937-130-2	£14.99	Peak District	1-85937-100-0	£14.99
Around Eastbourne	1-85937-061-6	£12.99	Around Penzance	1-85937-069-1	£12.99
Edinburgh (pb)	1-85937-193-0	£8.99	Around Plymouth	1-85937-119-1	£12.99

Available from your local bookshop or from the publisher

Frith Book Co Titles (continued)

Around Reading	1-85937-087-x	£12.99
Redhill to Reigate	1-85937-137-x	£12.99
Around St Ives	1-85937-068-3	£12.99
Around Salisbury	1-85937-091-8	£12.99
Around Scarborough	1-85937-104-3	£12.99
Scotland (pb)	1-85937-182-5	£9.99
Scottish Castles	1-85937-077-2	£14.99
Around Sevenoaks and Tonbridge		
	1-85937-057-8	£12.99
Sheffield and S Yorkshire	1-85937-070-5	£14.99
Around Southampton	1-85937-088-8	£12.99
Around Southport	1-85937-106-x	£12.99
Around Shrewsbury	1-85937-110-8	£12.99
Shropshire	1-85937-083-7	£14.99
South Devon Coast	1-85937-107-8	£14.99
South Devon Living Memories		
	1-85937-168-x	£14.99
Staffordshire (96pp)	1-85937-047-0	£12.99

Stone Circles & Ancient Monuments		
	1-85937-143-4	£17.99
Around Stratford upon Avon		
	1-85937-098-5	£12.99
Suffolk	1-85937-074-8	£14.99
Sussex (pb)	1-85937-184-1	£9.99
Surrey	1-85937-081-0	£14.99
Around Torbay	1-85937-063-2	£12.99
Around Truro	1-85937-147-7	£12.99
Victorian & Edwardian Kent		
	1-85937-149-3	£14.99
Victorian & Edwardian Yorkshire		
	1-85937-154-x	£14.99
Warwickshire (pb)	1-85937-203-1	£9.99
Welsh Castles	1-85937-120-5	£14.99
West Midlands	1-85937-109-4	£14.99
West Sussex	1-85937-148-5	£14.99
Wiltshire	1-85937-053-5	£14.99
Around Winchester	1-85937-139-6	£12.99

Frith Book Co titles available Autumn 2000

Croydon Living Memories (pb)			
	1-85937-162-0	£9.99	Aug
Glasgow (pb)	1-85937-190-6	£9.99	Aug
Hertfordshire (pb)	1-85937-247-3	£9.99	Aug
North London	1-85937-206-6	£14.99	Aug
Victorian & Edwardian Maritime Album			
	1-85937-144-2	£17.99	Aug
Victorian Seaside	1-85937-159-0	£17.99	Aug
Cornish Coast	1-85937-163-9	£14.99	Sep
County Durham	1-85937-123-x	£14.99	Sep
Dorset Living Memories	1-85937-210-4	£14.99	Sep
Gloucestershire	1-85937-102-7	£14.99	Sep
Herefordshire	1-85937-174-4	£14.99	Sep
Kent Living Memories	1-85937-125-6	£14.99	Sep
Leeds (pb)	1-85937-202-3	£9.99	Sep
Ludlow (pb)	1-85937-176-0	£9.99	Sep
Norfolk (pb)	1-85937-195-7	£9.99	Sep
Somerset	1-85937-153-1	£14.99	Sep
Tees Valley & Cleveland	1-85937-211-2	£14.99	Sep
Thanet (pb)	1-85937-116-7	£9.99	Sep
Tiverton (pb)	1-85937-178-7	£9.99	Sep
Weymouth (pb)	1-85937-209-0	£9.99	Sep

Worcestershire	1-85937-152-3	£14.99	Sep
Yorkshire Living Memories	1-85937-166-3	£14.99	Sep
British Life A Century Ago (pb)			
	1-85937-213-9	£9.99	Oct
Camberley (pb)	1-85937-222-8	£9.99	Oct
Cardiff (pb)	1-85937-093-4	£9.99	Oct
Carmarthenshire	1-85937-216-3	£14.99	Oct
Cornwall (pb)	1-85937-229-5	£9.99	Oct
County Maps of Britain	1-85937-156-6	£19.99	Oct
English Country Houses	1-85937-161-2	£17.99	Oct
Humberside	1-85937-215-5	£14.99	Oct
Lancashire (pb)	1-85937-197-3	£9.99	Oct
Manchester (pb)	1-85937-198-1	£9.99	Oct
Middlesex	1-85937-158-2	£14.99	Oct
Norfolk Living Memories	1-85937-217-1	£14.99	Oct
Preston (pb)	1-85937-212-0	£9.99	Oct
South Hams	1-85937-220-1	£14.99	Oct
Swansea (pb)	1-85937-167-1	£9.99	Oct
Victorian and Edwardian Sussex			
	1-85937-157-4	£14.99	Oct
West Yorkshire (pb)	1-85937-201-5	£9.99	Oct

See Frith books on the internet www.frithbook.co.uk

FRITH PRODUCTS & SERVICES

Francis Frith would doubtless be pleased to know that the pioneering publishing venture he started in 1860 still continues today. A hundred and forty years later, The Francis Frith Collection continues in the same innovative tradition and is now one of the foremost publishers of vintage photographs in the world. Some of the current activities include:

Interior Decoration

Today Frith's photographs can be seen framed and as giant wall murals in thousands of pubs, restaurants, hotels, banks, retail stores and other public buildings throughout the country. In every case they enhance the unique local atmosphere of the places they depict and provide reminders of gentler days in an increasingly busy and frenetic world.

Product Promotions

Frith products are used by many major companies to promote the sales of their own products or to reinforce their own history and heritage. Frith promotions have been used by Hovis bread, Courage beers, Scots Porage Oats, Colman's mustard, Cadbury's foods, Mellow Birds coffee, Dunhill pipe tobacco, Guinness, and Bulmer's Cider.

Genealogy and Family History

As the interest in family history and roots grows world-wide, more and more people are turning to Frith's photographs of Great Britain for images of the towns, villages and streets where their ancestors lived; and, of course, photographs of the churches and chapels where their ancestors were christened, married and buried are an essential part of every genealogy tree and family album.

Frith Products

All Frith photographs are available Framed or just as Mounted Prints and Posters (size 23 x 16 inches). These may be ordered from the address below. From time to time other products - Address Books, Calendars, Table Mats, etc - are available.

The Internet

Already twenty thousand Frith photographs can be viewed and purchased on the internet. By the end of the year 2000 some 60,000 Frith photographs will be available on the internet. The number of sites is constantly expanding, each focussing on different products and services from the Collection.

The main Frith sites are listed below.

www.francisfrith.co.uk

www.frithbook.co.uk

See the complete list of Frith Books at:

www.frithbook.co.uk

This web site is regularly updated with the latest list of publications from the Frith Book Company. If you wish to buy books relating to another part of the country that your local bookshop does not stock, you may purchase on-line.

For further information, trade, or author enquiries please contact us at the address below:
The Francis Frith Collection, Frith's Barn, Teffont, Salisbury, Wiltshire, England SP3 5QP.
Tel: +44 (0)1722 716 376 Fax: +44 (0)1722 716 881 Email: uksales@francisfrith.com

See Frith books on the internet www.frithbook.co.uk

TO RECEIVE YOUR FREE MOUNTED PRINT

Mounted Print
Overall size 14 x 11 inches

Cut out this Voucher and return it with your remittance for £1.50 to cover postage and handling, to UK addresses. For overseas addresses please include £4.00 post and handling. Choose any photograph included in this book. Your SEPIA print will be A4 in size, and mounted in a cream mount with burgundy rule lines, overall size 14 x 11 inches.

Order additional Mounted Prints at HALF PRICE (only £7.49 each*)

If there are further pictures you would like to order, possibly as gifts for friends and family, purchase them at half price (no additional postage and handling required).

Have your Mounted Prints framed*

For an additional £14.95 per print you can have your chosen Mounted Print framed in an elegant polished wood and gilt moulding, overall size 16 x 13 inches (no additional postage and handling required).

---

* IMPORTANT!
These special prices are only available if ordered using the original voucher on this page (no copies permitted) and at the same time as your free Mounted Print, for delivery to the same address

---

Frith Collectors' Guild

From time to time we publish a magazine of news and stories about Frith photographs and further special offers of Frith products. If you would like 12 months FREE membership, please return this form.

Send completed forms to:
The Francis Frith Collection, Frith's Barn, Teffont, Salisbury, Wiltshire SP3 5QP

Voucher for **FREE** and Reduced Price Frith Prints

Picture no.	Page number	Qty	Mounted @ £7.49	Framed + £14.95	Total Cost
		1	**Free of charge***	£	£
			£7.49	£	£
			£7.49	£	£
			£7.49	£	£
			£7.49	£	£
			£7.49	£	£

Please allow 28 days for delivery	*** Post & handling**	**£1.50**
Book Title	**Total Order Cost**	**£**

Please do not photocopy this voucher. Only the original is valid, so please cut it out and return it to us.

I enclose a cheque / postal order for £ . . . . made payable to 'The Francis Frith Collection'
OR please debit my Mastercard / Visa / Switch / Amex card

Number . . . .

Issue No(Switch only) . . . . .Valid from (Amex/Switch) . . . .

Expires . . . . Signature . . . .

Name Mr/Mrs/Ms . . . .

Address . . . .

. . . .

. . . .

. . . . Postcode . . . .

Daytime Tel No . . . .   Valid to 31/12/02

The Francis Frith Collectors' Guild
Please enrol me as a member for 12 months free of charge.

Name Mr/Mrs/Ms . . . .

Address . . . .

. . . .

. . . .

. . . . Postcode . . . .

Free Print - see overleaf